Cli

MW01714246

Goes to School

Created by
Norman Bridwell

SCHOLASTIC INC.

New York Toronto London Auckland
Sydney Mexico City New Delhi Hong Kong

Emily Elizabeth was leaving for school. "I'll see you when I get home," she told Clifford.

Oh no! Emily Elizabeth forgot her lunch!
Clifford decided to bring it to her.

Clifford looked for Emily Elizabeth in every classroom.

But he couldn't find her anywhere.

Emily Elizabeth was in the lunchroom.
Clifford found her just in time!

Clifford decided to stay for lunch.

He stayed for recess too.

"What would I do without you, Clifford?"
Emily Elizabeth gave her big dog a big hug.